IT'S YOUR DEAL

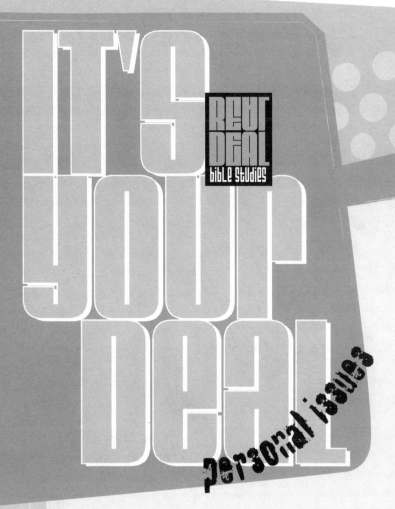

Real Deal bible studies

personal issues

AUTHORS

Beth Balzer

Tom Couser

Eric Dauber

Nathan Monke

Kevin Popp

Nikki Rochester

Mark Sengele

Harry Therwanger

Cynthia Werner

and Cindy Wheeler

EDITOR

Mark Sengele

CONCORDIA PUBLISHING HOUSE • SAINT LOUIS

Your comments and suggestions concerning the material are appreciated. Please write the Editor of Youth Materials, Concordia Publishing House, 3558 S. Jefferson Avenue, St. Louis, MO 63118-3968.

This publication may also be available in braille, in large print, or on cassette tape for the visually impaired. Please allow 8 to 12 weeks for delivery. Write to Library for the Blind, 1333 S. Kirkwood Road, St. Louis, MO 63122-7295; call 1-800-433-3954, ext. 1322; or e-mail to blind.library@lcms.org.

1 2 3 4 5 6 7 8 9 10   11 10 09 08 07 06 05 04 03 02

table of contents

iNTRODUCTION

Welcome to the Real Deal Series!

Welcome to the Real Deal! Each of the books in this series presents 12 lessons that focus on the Gospel and the Word of God, the Real Deal. Each book in the series has a theme around which the lessons are organized. (For an outline of the Real Deal Series, look inside the back cover of this book.)

* The **topics** are real. *Each lesson deals with real* issues in the lives of young people and is grounded in God's Word.

* The **leader's materials** are easy to use. *Each lesson is completely outlined and designed for real success in teaching. Leader's directions are clear and easy to follow. Materials needed for teaching are easily obtained. Many lessons contain additional materials for times when students finish quickly.*

* **Student pages** are reproducible so teachers can copy the number they really need.

* And, finally, the **power of the Gospel** is at the core of every study. Students will see God's Word as the real source of information for their everyday lives.

ABOUT THIS BOOK

It's Your Deal

Each of the 12 studies in this book deals with personal issues that many young people face. Many of these issues can be very sensitive for young people to deal with. Use care in your approach to each study so that God's truths remain objective and your care for each student becomes personalized.

The studies are designed for use with students in the ninth through twelfth grades. More mature junior high students may also benefit from these studies. Each study is a complete unit. Lessons may be used in any order. While designed for the typical one-hour Bible class, these studies may be adapted for other youth ministry settings. For example, selected studies could form the core of material for a youth night or retreat.

PREPARING TO TEACH

Each lesson has a *Lesson Focus* and a *Gospel Focus* statement at the beginning. These help the leader understand the lesson topic and direction.

The *Lesson Outline* provides a quick look at the study and a list of materials needed for each segment of the lesson.

The *Lesson Activities* include large and small group discussion, opportunities for individual study, and active-learning suggestions.

Most lessons also contain background information to assist the leader in preparing for the class time. Class leaders should review the entire lesson in advance of the class time.

It is assumed that the Bible class leader will have the usual basic classroom equipment and supplies available—pencils or pens for each student, blank paper (and occasionally tape or marking pens), and a chalkboard or its equivalent (white board, overhead transparency projector, or newsprint pad and easel) with corresponding markers or chalk. Encourage the students to bring their own Bibles. Then they can mark useful passages and make notes to guide their personal Bible study and reference. Provide additional Bibles, however, for visitors or students who do not bring one. The appropriate Student Page should be copied in a quantity sufficient for the class and distributed at the time indicated in the leader's notes.

The studies are outlined completely in the leader's notes, including a suggested length of time for each section of the study. The suggested times will total 50–55 minutes, the maximum amount most Sunday morning Bible classes have available. Each session begins with an opening activity that may or may not be indicated on the Student Page. Teachers who regularly begin with prayer should include it before the opening activity. Most other parts of the study, except the closing prayer, are indicated on both the Leader Page and Student Page.

An average class size of 10 students is assumed. To facilitate discussion, especially when your class is larger than average, it is recommended to conduct much of the discussion in smaller groups—pairs, triads, or groups of no more than five or six. Instructions to that effect are often included in the guide. If your class is small, you are already a small group and can ignore any such suggestions.

Some lessons contain bonus suggestions. Use these when the study progresses more quickly than expected, when your normal session exceeds 50–55 minutes, or when a suggested activity doesn't work with your group. They can also be used during the week.

Of course, the leader is encouraged to review the study thoroughly, well in advance of its presentation. Then the materials can be tailored to your individual students' needs and preferences as well as your own preferred teaching style.

TIPS FOR LEADERS OF YOUTH BIBLE STUDIES

One challenge of leading a youth Bible study is the need for relevant, Christ-centered, effective study material. An equal challenge is growing in one's ability to teach and lead effectively. While the studies in the Real Deal Series are intended to meet the first challenge, these next six points are intended to help you meet the second challenge.

Skim this section for ideas that spark your interest, or read it completely. Either way, you'll find support to help young people grow in God's Word.

SIX BASIC SKILLS FOR TEACHERS (AND HOW TO GROW IN THEM)

Teaching Is a Skill That Can Be Learned

Some would say that teaching is a gift. Paul lists it among the spiritual gifts that God gives for the building up of the saints. Some might say that it is a talent or art. To be sure, many people are at ease in a teaching role, gifted in speaking to groups, and at home in class-room settings.

Teaching is a gift, it is a talent or art, but it is also a skill or set of skills that can be learned and improved through study and practice. Those who want to improve their teaching skills could strive to incorporate the following six *basic teaching skills*: (1) distinguishing Law and Gospel, (2) choosing concepts, (3) choosing objectives, (4) developing a teaching strategy, (5) guiding classroom interaction, and (6) using a variety of media. Each of these areas is described further in the material that follows, and some suggestions for further study are offered.

1. Distinguishing Law and Gospel

No skill is more critical for the effective teaching of God's Word than teaching properly God's Law and Gospel. The ultimate goal of Bible study is to change the lives of those who study God's Word. Life change comes about as God works in the hearts of His people through His Word as Law and as Gospel. The Law shows us our sin and brings about the realization that no human effort or worldly power can make us right with God or able to please Him. The Gospel reveals the Savior Jesus Christ to us, as God's Holy Spirit works saving faith in our hearts to believe that Jesus suffered and died to pay for our sin. The Holy Spirit works repentance for our sin and creates in us new life and power to live for Him.

The Gospel cannot do the work of the Law. If we do not see our sin, we have no need for a Savior. If we heard no Law, we would be callous toward God's great grace and mercy, lax in our devotion, and indifferent to God's will for us.

Neither can the Law do the work of the Gospel. The Law can motivate us through fear, but it cannot change our sinful hearts. Good works done in response to the Law will always fall short of the perfection the Law requires. Without the Gospel we remain mired in our sin, resentful of God and His Word, and unable to share joyfully in His work.

In both our *justification*, our coming to faith in Jesus through the power of the Holy Spirit, and in our *sanctification*, our growing more mature as a spiritual creation of God, the Law and Gospel do their work. A teacher does well to teach them clearly and to not get them confused.

A classic work in this area is *The Proper Distinction of Law and Gospel* by C. F. W. Walther, a Lutheran theologian of the nineteenth century. This book, containing lecture notes on the topic of Law and Gospel, is available through Concordia Publishing House for your personal reading and study.

2. Choosing Concepts

Choosing concepts for study refers to selecting the subjects to be studied and identifying how much the students know about them. Students, especially young people, respond poorly to material (1) that fails to challenge them or that they "already know," (2) that is too far beyond their present level of understanding, or (3) that seems irrelevant to their lives. These extremes can be avoided by careful selection and adaptation of material.

Several avenues for growth have potential:

* *In consultation with your pastor, superintendent, or board of Christian education, set long-term goals for the youth Bible-study programs in your congregation. What areas of study seem important and why? Where could the*

students be a year from now? Consider behavioral goals (what should the students be doing?) and affective goals (what should be the students' attitudes and feelings?) as well as cognitive goals (what should the students know?).

* *Stay in touch with the world of young people and their culture. Occasionally read a magazine, watch a television program, listen to a radio station, or see a movie that is popular among the youth you serve. Borrow or subscribe to a periodical or two that keeps abreast of trends in youth culture.*

* *Know the youth that you teach. Talk to them, and listen to them talk to you and to each other. Let them evaluate the material you teach or the material you consider teaching.*

3. Choosing and Sequencing Objectives

Objectives are the specific results you desire to obtain after you have taught a particular lesson. They guide the lesson outline. They are the small steps that make up the longer journey toward your goals. They are a tool for evaluating each lesson for its impact and for future teaching.

Objectives are best written in terms of *student activity* (not "I will teach" but rather "the students will describe"). Objectives benefit from being *observable* (not "will know" or "will feel," which are internal, but "will tell about" or "will give thanks for," which are external). Also beneficial is developing objectives that are measurable and attainable.

Your students are a unique set of people with their own needs, knowledge, and interests. The best lessons will be those that you have tailored to suit them. In published material, you the teacher should become familiar with the objectives that are printed, adjust them if necessary for your group, or choose which one or two to emphasize and adjust the lesson as necessary. In lessons you construct on your own, be careful to limit your objectives. In one hour it is unlikely that more than two or three objectives can be fully accomplished. Give attention as well to the sequence in which the objectives are taught; logic generally suggests an "information, analysis, application" order to things.

4. Developing a Teaching Strategy

A teaching strategy is a plan of activities and materials that the teacher uses to accomplish objectives and reach goals. It is the lesson plan that is prepared to map out the class time for you and answer questions such as the following:

* *How will I gain the students' attention?*

* *How will their need for this study be revealed?*

* *How will relevant information be shared?*

* *What portions of the Bible will be studied? How will this be done?*

* *How will Scripture be applied to the students' lives?*

How will changes in the students' lives be suggested as a result of the study?

A good strategy will flow from one part to the next. Your lesson plan might even include the transition sentences you use. A good strategy will include a variety of activities that will appeal to the students (possibly including things such as small-group discussion and active-learning activities). It will exhibit variety from week to week to prevent staleness. It will accomplish the objectives in a logical sequence and, with God's help, result in changed lives.

Since the students you teach are unique, a published lesson outline may benefit from adaptation to best serve them. Substitute activities that they will enjoy more, choose to ask and answer the questions you know they will have, and use other resources you have on hand. Creativity in this area is a tremendous plus!

5. Guiding Classroom Interaction

Classroom interaction includes everything that takes place between teacher and student, student and student, and student and materials in the course of a lesson. An effective teacher is aware of these interactions as they take place and to some degree can control them through effective instructions, appropriate questions, and on-the-spot adaptations of the teaching strategy.

6. Using a Variety of Media

A final critical skill for teachers is the use of media. Young people generally respond positively to variety in this area. Data projectors, recorded music, video, crafts, puppets, drama, pictures and posters, puzzles and games, and an endless variety of other media are available for use in your classroom. As you make the effort to experiment with and learn to use these tools, students' interest will likely increase along with the amount of learning that takes place.

Educational media workshops are sometimes available through your church, the local library, a community college, or other institutions. Observe the way other teachers make use of different media tools. Borrow ideas and resources freely from other teachers and other grade levels. While some activities intended for older groups are too complex for younger children, very few activities are too simple for older groups to enjoy and find beneficial.

PERMANENT MARKERS

LESSON FOCUS

Body modification—including tattooing, piercing, branding, scarification, and other forms—holds a curious attraction for young people. Some call it a form of neo-tribalism—an effort to reconnect with one's cultural identity or heritage. For others it serves as a rite of passage from adolescence to young adulthood. Still others see it as a form of self-expression, a declaration of individuality. Whatever the reason, body modification is a growing trend among young people. Many of these are not kids living on the edge or as part of some urban subculture; rather they are middle-class, church-going, suburban teenagers.

GOSPEL FOCUS

Teens need to understand that their bodies are not their own. 1 Corinthians 6 reminds us that our bodies are "members of Christ Himself" (verse 15) and that we were "bought at a price," and therefore we "honor God with [our] bodies" (verse 20). Through the price that Christ paid on the cross, we receive forgiveness and the promise of eternal life.

Lesson Outline

ACTIVITY	SUGGESTED TIME	MATERIALS NEEDED
Identifying Marks	10 minutes	Pictures as described in lesson
Markers	15 minutes	Copies of Student Page
Leaving His Mark on Me	15 minutes	None
Closing ReMarks	10 minutes	None

BEFORE YOU BEGIN

Body modification is a broad term for a number of different forms of decorating the human body. These include tattooing, piercing, branding, scarification, and others. Tattoos are created by inserting ink deep into the skin using a needle or tattoo gun to produce a picture or design. Piercing commonly involves placing metal (sometimes glass) jewelry through holes pierced in the face and ears. In recent years the piercing of the nipples, navel, tongue, and/or genitals has also become popular. Branding involves "striking" a white-hot metal branding iron on the flesh one or more times in order to produce a design. Scarification results from cutting the skin in a pattern to produce a raised scar.

While many piercings will close up again and some tattoos can be removed with laser or other surgery, the majority of body modifications become permanent marks upon the skin. In addition, health officials express serious concerns about the spread of blood-borne diseases (especially hepatitis) through the explosion of this trend.

IDENTIFYING MARKS (10 MINUTES)

Distribute photos of people in easily identified uniforms or costumes. Ask students what the clothing suggests about each individual. Next share a picture of someone with body modifications, or ask students if they know anyone personally who has a tattoo, piercing, or the like. Ask, "What does the distinct body modification suggest to you about this person?" Lead students to understand that body modifications communicate a message, in much the same way that wearing a uniform or other articles of clothing does. Survey students to find out how much they already know about body modification. Share appropriate information from the "Before You Begin" section with your students.

MARKERS (15 MINUTES)

Distribute copies of the Student Page. Assign students to work together in small groups to look up the Scripture passages listed. Different passages talk about different kinds of marks. Ask groups to summarize each passage for the whole group and identify what the "mark" was intended to communicate. Use the following notes as you lead a discussion with students.

Genesis 4:10–16—After being confronted with the murder of his brother, Cain is marked by God so that others will know not to kill him. While we do not know what kind of mark this is, it somehow communicates to others that they are to leave Cain alone. The mark will tell others of Cain's sin but is intended by God to protect Cain.

Genesis 17:9–14—God commands Abraham and his (male) descendants to be circumcised as a physical sign of the covenant between God and His chosen people. Jewish males were marked in this way eight days after they were born. Circumcision served as a constant reminder of their covenant relationship with God. (You may wish to remind students that circumcision is still required for all males in both the Jewish and Islamic faiths. While not required for Christians, circumcision is routinely performed for hygienic or personal preference reasons.)

Genesis 24:22, 28–31, 47–51—Abraham's servant gives Rebekah a golden nose ring (and other jewelry) as a gift. The ring identifies Rebekah as the chosen bride for Isaac. The wearing of a nose ring by married women is common in many eastern societies.

Exodus 21:2–6; Deuteronomy 15:16–17—Hebrew servants who voluntarily stayed with their masters after the seventh year, when they could go free, were marked by their master. This marking was accomplished by piercing their ear with an awl against the door or door frame. This piercing symbolized the servant's voluntary loyalty and understanding that life as a slave to a kind master was often better than freedom in abject poverty.

Revelation 13:16–18; 20:4—The followers of the beast are marked with his number upon their hand or forehead. This mark most likely makes reference to pagan religious tattoos worn by first-century people. It was a symbol of loyalty to evil.

Caution students that none of these biblical examples justifies body modifications in our contemporary society. Students are not being encouraged to rationalize body modification in their discussion with parents or other adults.

LEAVING HIS MARK ON ME (15 MINUTES)

Ask a volunteer to read aloud Psalm 40:5–6. In this psalm David recalls God's past mercies. David refers to the practice of a master piercing a servant's ear when he says to God "but my ears You have pierced" (verse 6). While David's ears were probably not literally pierced, these words remind David of his voluntary service to God. David could have afforded any number of offerings to God, but what God desired was David's loyal heart and complete service.

Read together Isaiah 53:5. In these words Isaiah prophesies the price that Christ would pay for our salvation. Through the piercing of Christ's flesh and the sacrificial pouring out of His own blood, we are made clean. Through faith we receive Christ's free gift of salvation and the promise of eternal life with Him.

Have students read Galatians 6:12–17 and Colossians 2:9–12. Paul tells the Galatian Christians that the outward mark of circumcision is not required for followers of Christ, calling those who require it "mutilators of the flesh" (Philippians 3:2). Instead Baptism has become the mark of God's covenant with His chosen people. Through Baptism we are buried with Christ and raised again with Him to eternal life.

God places His mark on us at our Baptism, and our lives become transformed. The heavenly Father declares us to be His own beloved children (1 John 3:1). Our faith continues to be strengthened and nurtured through the study of God's Word and participation in the Sacraments.

CLOSING REMARKS (10 MINUTES)

God's children represent Him on earth. In his letter to the church at Corinth, Paul reminds us that our bodies are "members of Christ Himself" (1 Corinthians 6:15). Help students understand the kinds of messages that they communicate about themselves—and about Christ—through their appearance. Through the power of the Holy Spirit, God helps us make decisions that please Him. Close with prayer, thanking God for His gift of faith and eternal life. Include any special prayer concerns that students may share.

I. PERMANENT MARKERS

MARKERS

Look at the verses that follow.
What does each tell about the marks placed on the person?

Genesis 4:10–16

Genesis 17:9–14

Genesis 24:22, 28–31, 47–51

Exodus 21:2–6; Deuteronomy 15:16–17

Revelation 13:16–18; 20:4

Leaving his mark on me

What does each of these verses say about the mark that God places on us?

Psalm 40:5–6

Isaiah 53:5

Galatians 6:12–17

Colossians 2:9–12

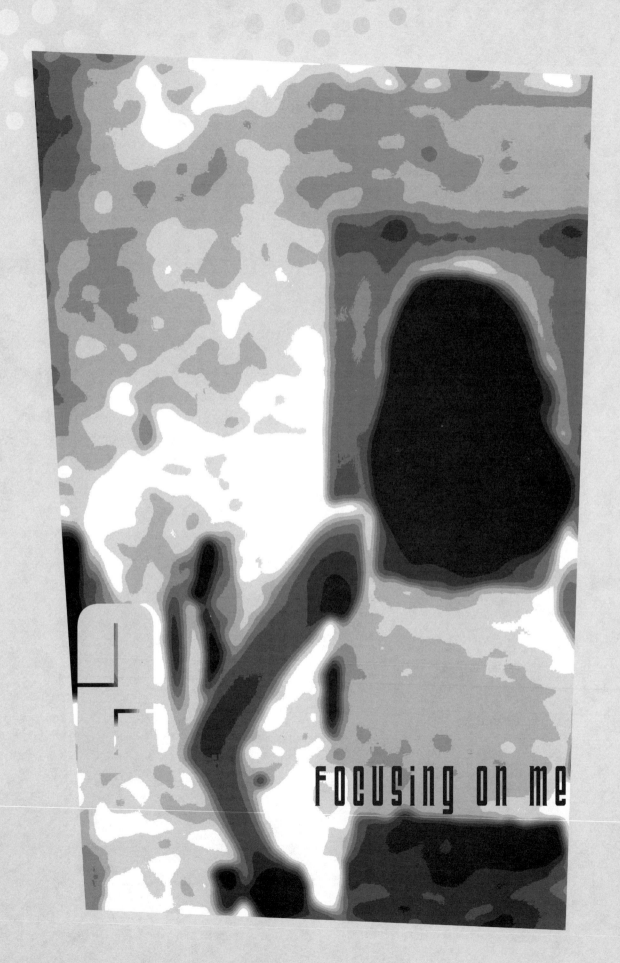

focusing on me

LESSON FOCUS

Young people often have a distorted view of themselves, caused in part by the world's obsession with outward appearance. Devaluing oneself and others does not honor God. Young people must learn to focus not on *who* they are, but rather on *whose* they are.

GOSPEL FOCUS

Healthy self-esteem rests upon the assurance of God's love as revealed in Scripture. God loves each of us personally, intimately, and deeply. He demonstrated this love by creating and redeeming us through Jesus Christ. His love and forgiveness enable us to offer these same gifts to others.

Lesson Outline

ACTIVITY	SUGGESTED TIME	MATERIALS NEEDED
Focus the Picture	*5 minutes*	*Copies of Student Page, index cards*
Take a Look	*10 minutes*	*Index cards*
Polish the Lens	*15 minutes*	*Copies of Student Page*
Try a New Lens	*15 minutes*	*Bibles, copies of Student Page, newsprint, markers*
Replay the New Vision	*5 minutes*	*Index cards*
Closing	*2 minutes*	*None*
Bonus Activity	*10 minutes*	*Advertisements from newspapers and magazines*

FOCUS THE PICTURE (5 MINUTES)

Divide students into small groups. Ask one student from each group to serve as the facilitator. Give each student an index card and a copy of the Student Page.

Direct the attention of the group to the questions in this section of the Student Page. Invite participants to write 10 words that describe themselves on the index card.

Have them do this privately. Ask students not to share their work at this time.

TAKE A LOOK (10 MINUTES)

This is an individual activity. No sharing should be required. When most of the students have completed their lists, say something such as, "The words you listed say something about your 'me-vision'—how you see yourself."

Ask students to identify the descriptions on their list with one or more of the following marks (write these marks on newsprint or the chalkboard):

+	if it is positive
-	if it is negative
A	if it describes activities (writer, athlete, etc.)
R	if it describes roles you play (daughter, friend, etc.)
Q	if it describes personality characteristics (playful, sincere, etc.)
P	if it describes physical characteristics (tall, blond, etc.)

Allow time for this step. Invite further personal reflection by asking students the following questions:

"Is your list mostly positive or mostly negative?"

"Does it mostly describe activities, roles, personality characteristics, or physical characteristics?"

"What could this indicate about your 'me-vision'?"

POLISH THE LENS (15 MINUTES)

Direct students to the sentence starters found in this section of the Student Page. Remind them that they will be asked to share at least one of the completed sentences with the others in their small group. When the small groups have finished, invite volunteers to share with the whole group what these activities have taught them about themselves.

TRY A NEW LENS (15 MINUTES)

Direct the groups to this Bible study. Assign two or more passages to each group. Ask students to look up these verses. Have them complete the phrases on the Student Page based on what they read.

Have the groups discuss each of the questions in this section, reflecting on their Scripture passages. Provide each group with newsprint and markers. Have a member from each small group record the responses from their group. Then review the responses as a whole group.

Affirm God's value for each individual as His unique creation. He knows each of them intimately. His Son has redeemed them. They are called by name and made members of His family by faith.

Stress the changes the Holy Spirit works in us through Word and Sacraments. He motivates and energizes us to respond to God's goodness by valuing others and showing our love for them.

Bonus Activity: *Gather a variety of advertisements clipped from newspapers and magazines that display our society's obsession with appearance. Share the pictures with your class. Ask, "Do you or people you know feel pressure to conform to these images of beauty? Why? What things do people do to improve their appearance? What would God say to us about our concern over external appearances?"*

REPLAY THE NEW VISION (5 MINUTES)

Say, "Select one of the sentence starters. Write it on the other side of your index card from the beginning of our study. Share your response with your small group. Then take it home with you. Put it where you will see it often (a mirror, backpack, etc.). Let it remind you of the new vision that is yours through Jesus Christ, who died for you and rose again." Allow time for sharing.

CLOSING (2 MINUTES)

Close with a circle prayer. Invite students to think about something they like about themselves and to thank God for it. End the prayer with a statement of gratitude to God for the new people you have become through faith in Christ Jesus.

2. Focusing on Me

Focus the Picture

Pretend you are looking at yourself through the lens of a video camera.
What do you see? How would you describe yourself to someone you've never met?

Polish the Lens

Summarize what you've said about yourself by completing these sentences.
Plan to share at least one with the group.

Who am I? I am . . .

Who influences me? Other people tell me I am . . .

What do I value? I think it is important to . . .

Try a New Lens

Write responses in the columns below using the following Scripture passages:

Scripture	God Thinks I Am . . .	Because . . .
Genesis 1:27, 31		
Psalm 139:13–14		
Romans 3:21–24		
Isaiah 43:1		
Galatians 3:26–29		

self-image

Whom does God say I am?

What does God value about me?

How does this view differ from my previous responses?

How can God's view change my view of myself?

How can God's view change my view of other people?

Since God loves and accepts me, what can I offer others?

REPLAY the NEW VISION

The Bible says I am _____.

Jesus thinks I'm special because _____.

Because God loves me, I can _____.

I'm not _____. I'm _____ in God's eyes!

19

3

FUTURE POTENTIAL

LESSON FOCUS

Thinking about the future can be intimidating for anyone. Young people especially may feel anxiety as they strive to balance pressing needs and face major decisions about college, career, family, and future.

GOSPEL FOCUS

God's plan is always to bless, to give the best possible results. We sin when we replace His goals for us with our own and when we seek to accomplish His goals through our own efforts. God promises complete forgiveness for these failures through faith in Jesus' sacrifice. By the power of the Holy Spirit working through Word and Sacraments, God enables our plans to be rooted in Him.

LESSON OUTLINE

ACTIVITY	SUGGESTED TIME	MATERIALS NEEDED
Opening	10 minutes	Dart gun, ring toss, or similar aiming toy; blindfold
Drawing a Map	15 minutes	Copies of Student Page
His Map for Me	15 minutes	Copies of Student Page, Bibles
Getting Personal	10 minutes	Chalkboard or newsprint
Praying about the Future	5 minutes	None

OPENING (10 MINUTES)

Challenge students to test their aim with a suction dart board, ring toss, Nerf basketball, or similar activity. When everyone has had a chance, ask for volunteers to try the same activity blindfolded.

Or ask students to share about a time they were traveling in an unfamiliar place without a map or to imagine what such an experience would be like.

DRAWING A MAP (15 MINUTES)

Distribute copies of the Student Page. Point out that often people go through life without goals, which is similar to aiming blindly or going on a journey without a map. Let the students begin to sketch a map for their future as they fill in the sentences on the Student Page. Allow time for them to share their answers. Have students break into groups of three to five. After allowing 10 minutes to share, gather the whole group again and ask how many students were able to fill in all the blanks. Point out that some people may not have their map of life completely drawn yet. Ask each student to choose one dream they worry about achieving (e.g., having enough money to go to college, finding a job they like, having enough talent to accomplish a particular goal). Ask them to share their concern in their small group and to discuss why they have these worries. Ask them to share how these worries affect their ability to achieve their dreams.

HIS MAP FOR ME (15 MINUTES)

Ask students, "Do you believe that God has a specific map for your lives, including the details of where you will live and work and whom you will marry?" Point out that some Christians believe that God's map is very specific, while others believe His map for us involves simply that we live as Christians in whatever course our life takes.

The Bible is the most certain map that God has provided for all Christians, as it shows the way to salvation. Ask students to look up the verses on the Student Page to get some glimpses of God's map for their future. Discuss the questions that follow each verse. If the group is large, divide into smaller groups and assign one verse to each group.

The following notes will help as you discuss the questions.

Jeremiah 29:1–14—What kind of plans does God have for these people and for us? Whose lies are the people not to listen to? Where might you hear lies about your future and the map for your life? *God speaks to the exiled children of Israel in Babylon. The message to them and to us is that God's plans give us hope and a future (verse 11). The world often paints a false picture concerning the important things in life, which can cause us to despair about our future.*

Luke 12:6–7, 22–34—How much does God know about our future? What do these verses say about the worries we have? *God knows every detail of our lives. Our worries about the future prove pointless and unproductive because God graciously provides for us.*

Psalm 37:1–11—What do you think these verses say about God's plan for us? *When our greatest desire is for the Lord, God adds the desires of our heart.*

Ask the group to summarize God's map for their future in a sentence or two based on these verses. Emphasize that God works in each of us through the Holy Spirit because of God's love for us in Christ Jesus. He directs our decisions and also moves us to do His will in our circumstances. We can count on four things:

1. We will not always choose our goals correctly due to our sinful human nature. God sent Jesus to earn our forgiveness for all such failures.

2. God's will in our lives does not always include success and good times. He works for our good and the good of others, often through trial and tribulation. Hard times do not mean we have set the wrong goals or acted contrary to God's will.

3. God will not abandon us. He patiently continues to work in our lives by His grace, despite our sin.

4. God can make all things work together for good to those who love God and are called according to His purpose.

GETTING PERSONAL (10 MINUTES)

We use God's plan as we map out a personal plan for our lives. Ask each student to choose one of their dreams listed earlier in the session. Write *M A P* vertically on a chalkboard or newsprint. Urge them to write one specific personal goal that is *Measurable, Achievable,* and *Pleasing to God*. Write these words after the corresponding letter and explain each of the principles. For example, "I want to get a good scholarship" is not a measurable goal. *Good* is too abstract. "I plan to have at least half of my tuition at the state university paid by an athletic scholarship" is *measurable*. "I will earn $100,000 per year at my first job" and "I will marry a movie star" are probably not *achievable* goals. Finally, challenge students to think about whether the goal they have for themselves pleases God. Does it use the talents He has given him or her? Does it follow His will? Give the students a few minutes to write their MAP on the back of the Student Page. Ask volunteers to share their MAP.

PRAYING ABOUT THE FUTURE (5 MINUTES)

Close in prayer, thanking God for the gracious plan He has for each of us. Ask His forgiveness for the times we lack trust in His plan and worry about the future. Allow time for students to pray individually about their plans (silently or aloud). They may want to ask for God's help in achieving their goals and His guidance in making their plans.

3. Future Potential

drawing a map

Fill in each of the following sentences with your dreams for the future.

1. If I go to college, I would like to go to _____ and major in

_____.

2. My ideal job would be as a _____ earning _____ per year.

3. Three qualities I am looking for in a mate are_____

_____ and _____. We would have _____ children.

4. If I could choose anywhere in the world, I would live in _____.

5. A hobby I would like to pursue someday is _____.

6. Three qualities I would look for in choosing a church to attend are

_____ _____ and _____.

7. One thing I would like to accomplish before I'm 30 is

_____.

his map for me

Jeremiah 29:1–14—*What kind of plans does God have for these people and for us? Whose lies are the people not to listen to? Where might you hear lies about your future and the map for your life?*

Luke 12:6–7, 22–34—*How much does God know about our future? What do these verses say about the worries we have?*

Psalm 37:1–11—*What do you think these verses say about God's plan for us?*

getting personal

Choose one of the dreams above and write a specific goal for yourself. Make sure the MAP you draw is Measurable, Achievable, and Pleasing to God.

if i only had a brain

LESSON FOCUS

Young people grow in independence, especially as they emerge from their reliance on parents. Many appear to reject the wisdom and guidance of their parents as they depend upon the approval of their peers for input on decisions. As they grow through this study of God's Word, young people can confidently learn better to discern good from bad as God helps them reject faulty human resources and rely on His fault-less wisdom.

GOSPEL FOCUS

The growing independence of young people is part of God's plan. Rather than rejecting the biblical authority of their parents and following the group culture of their peers, young Christians can be directed to the resources that God provides for strengthening their faith—His Word and Sacraments.

Lesson Outline

ACTIVITY	SUGGESTED TIME	MATERIALS NEEDED
Opening	10 minutes	Buttons and box
What Scripture Says	20 minutes	Copies of Student Page
Conform or Be Transformed?	15 minutes	Copies of Student Page
Closing	10 minutes	Newsprint

BACKGROUND FOR THE LEADER

Throughout the Gospels Jesus teaches using many parables that require His listeners to think in order to understand what He is trying to convey. Jesus challenges individuals to use their God-given minds in order to understand Him. "He who has ears to hear, let him hear" (Mark 4:9).

Rather than using our own intellects to further our mental and spiritual growth, it appears easier to let someone else do our thinking and perhaps even make our decisions for us. Initially this may be less painful, and mistakes can be blamed on others.

But God has given us a brain and expects each of us to use it. God desires that we use our mind to serve Him so that His purposes might be fulfilled.

OPENING (10 MINUTES)

Play *Buttons*. Choose and instruct a volunteer as described below. Place 10 or more buttons (coins or other objects) in a box with a lid, and pass the box around the group. Each person silently counts the objects and passes the box to the next person. Unknown to the last person or to the rest of the group, the second to last person removes one object (the leader arranges this beforehand).

Begin with the first counter and have each person in sequence share the number of objects he or she counted. Chances are great that the last person will report the same number everyone else did. Explain the set-up to the group. Ask the last person why he or she did or did not report the same number as the rest of the group. Ask, "How did it feel to go along with or go against the crowd? Was it hard to decide what answer to give? What would the rest of you have done?"

WHAT SCRIPTURE SAYS (20 MINUTES)

Distribute copies of the Student Page. Allow students to complete this section individually. Then direct them to share their responses in small groups of three to five. After about 10 minutes, invite sample responses from each small group. Allow any answer to the first three questions, but encourage each person to explain his or her reason for that answer.

Make it clear to the students that the power for Christlike living comes from Christ Himself, by the Holy Spirit working through our Baptism and God's Word. 1 Peter 4:1 makes this implication, which is more clearly stated in 1 Peter 3:18: "For Christ died for sins once for all, the righteous for the unrighteous, to bring you to God." As God's people we have the power of Christ at work in us. The next section will reemphasize this idea.

CONFORM OR BE TRANSFORMED? (15 MINUTES)

Ask, "Do you think life was really different from how it is today or temptations easier in biblical times than now? What might Christ's thoughts have been while He was being tempted? What might God's purposes be? How do you know? Where does Scripture fit in? If the Scriptures are important because God speaks through them, why aren't we more eager to attend Bible studies?" *Accept reasonable answers. Christ was tempted in the same way we are, but He remained sinless. We can only know God's pur-*

poses through what we are told in His Word.

Read Romans 12:2 and the introductory paragraph for this section. Direct the students to mark responses, and invite volunteers to talk about the general areas in which they find it difficult to be transformed. Point out that the transformation process described by Paul is hindered by sin. Our sinful neglect of God's Word and reliance on sources of worldly wisdom will guide us in the wrong direction. We grow in our ability to resist temptation as we hear and study God's Word, share in the Sacraments, and confess and receive forgiveness for our sins.

CLOSING (10 MINUTES)

Write the following prayer formula on newsprint, chalkboard, or marker board for all to see.

"Lord, send your Spirit to transform my mind from being . . . so that I can . . ."

Allow time for individuals to write a prayer based on the formula on the back of the Student Page or on blank paper. Invite volunteers to share their prayers as the closing prayer. Allow a time of silence for the others to pray their prayer silently.

4. if i ONLY had a brain

WHAT SCRIPTURE SAYS

Read 1 Peter 4:1–4.

1. In **verse 1** *having the same attitude as Christ means*

___ *not thinking for myself.*

___ *to be considered a fool.*

___ *impossible.*

___ *to live as Christ's disciple.*

___ *other:* _____.

2. *Living for the will of God (**verse 2**) is difficult because*

___ *there are too many temptations.*

___ *I don't know what God's will is.*

___ *it may cause some hardship.*

___ *I don't want to.*

___ *other:* _____.

3. *It would be easy to become involved in the lifestyles mentioned in **verses 3–4** because*

___ *it seems that everybody else does it.*

___ *I am encouraged by* _____ *to be involved.*

___ *there isn't much discouragement not to become involved.*

___ *it is a natural part of growing up.*

___ *other:* _____.

4. *What power do we have to avoid these sins and all sinful actions?*
*(See **1 Peter 3:18.**)*

decision making

CONFORM OR BE TRANSFORMED?

*Read **Romans 12:2**.*

Do you generally conform to outside influence?
In which of the following areas is it most difficult for you to resist conforming to worldly ways?

___ leisure time   ___ career plan   ___ books/magazines

___ dress/looks   ___ lifestyle   ___ music

___ habits   ___ attitudes   ___ possessions

___ speech   ___ values   ___ school

God would have an easier time transforming my mind if

___ *I would tune in to His will through His Word.*

___ *I would think through my actions before I did them.*

___ *I would put my beliefs into action.*

___ *I would act more on the basis of Christ's acceptance of me*

     and less on the basis of my friends' approval.

___ _____. *(Add your own.)*

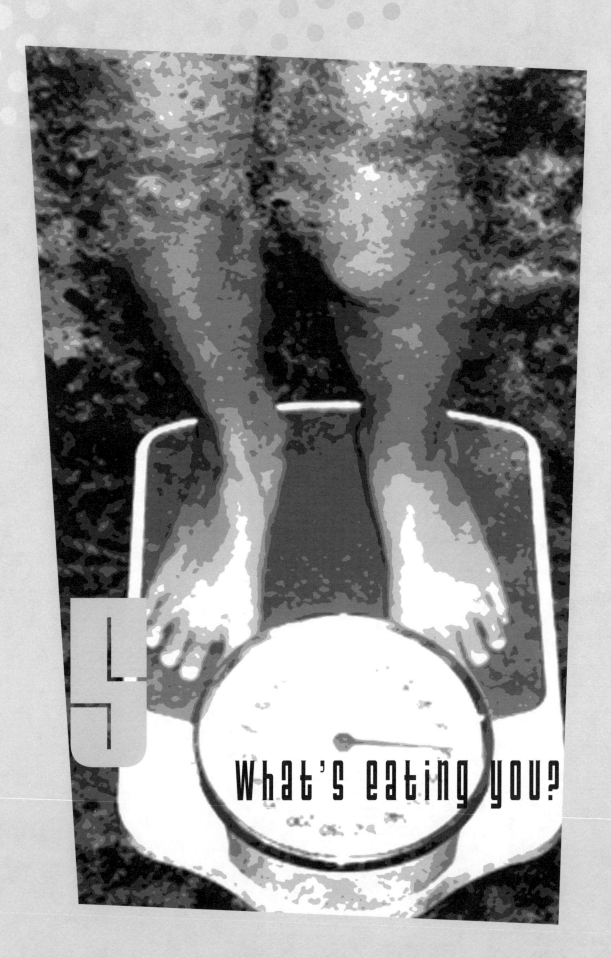

What's eating you?

LESSON FOCUS

Eating disorders affect many teens, personally or through friends or acquaintances. The Internet hosts a number of anorexia/bulimia support groups. Young people are confused and overwhelmed by changes that occur with their bodies during the teenage years. Many adolescents underestimate the body's need for certain basic habits.

GOSPEL FOCUS

Eating disorders are an outgrowth of sin, as Satan and the world attack a person's perception of himself or herself as a valued creation of God. As young people learn about eating disorders and about God's love for them as shown in the suffering, death, and resurrection of Jesus Christ on their behalf, they are equipped by the power of the Spirit to resist assaults on their self-esteem and to help others as they express their faith.

Lesson Outline

ACTIVITY	SUGGESTED TIME	MATERIALS NEEDED
Opening	10 minutes	None
What Would You Do If . . . ?	10 minutes	Copies of Student Page
Eating Disorders	10 minutes	Leader's notes
God's Word	20 minutes	Copies of Student Page
Closing	5 minutes	None

BEFORE YOU BEGIN

The subject of eating disorders may be a sensitive issue for some of your students. Acquaint yourself with information concerning eating disorders before you begin the lesson. Information should be available through your local health department or school system. You may want to invite a medical professional with experience in dealing with eating disorders to speak with the students. Be sure to find out what treatment resources are available in your community.

OPENING (10 MINUTES)

Invite two volunteers to role-play a mom and/or dad trying to get a five-year-old to eat all of a dinner of liver and spinach.

Or discuss favorite foods or junk foods. "How hard are they to resist? What if you could have all of the food you wanted? How much and how long could you keep eating? When and why would you stop?"

Then say, "Our eating habits, likes, and dislikes are sometimes difficult to control. Have you ever been so full at a big meal—say Thanksgiving—that you wanted to vomit for release? Sometimes our eating habits can create feelings of frustration at not being in control, embarrassment over appearance, and endless cycles of weight loss and gain. For some, obsession over appearance or a distorted self-view may create clinical eating disorders."

Ask, "Have you, or has anyone you know, ever vomited to feel better or to keep a certain weight or appearance? What would motivate that behavior? How might one feel before and after?" (Pause for responses.)

Continue, "Some people have those feelings often. They may need help to deal with these feelings. It could be some people here at church or some of your friends at school or even your own family members. Would you recognize the signs?"

WHAT WOULD YOU DO IF . . . ? (10 MINUTES)

Distribute copies of the Student Page. Lead the students to briefly discuss the case studies. If the size of your group allows, assign each case study to a different group of three to five students.

EATING DISORDERS (10 MINUTES)

Supplement the Student Page with the following information.

* *Food Addiction (Obesity)—Each of us inherits a set of genetic rules that will influence our basic makeup, inclinations, and choices. Your best weight is your best weight, that which is healthiest for you.*

* *Fat/Thin Disorder—Many people identify food as the cause of emotional pain or distress and seek healing or solace through eating more or less food. However, instead of the food becoming the path to deal with difficult emotions, the constant thoughts about food divert emotional energy from more productive problem solving, thoughts, and skills.*

* *Anorexia Nervosa—Even as they waste away, anorexics see themselves as fat or ugly. Young women ages 13–25 seem most susceptible to this condition.*

* *Bulimia—When the dieting or starvation fails to produce the desired weight loss or appearance, or when the person fails to control the appetite for food, she induces vomiting to purge the food she has ingested. Like anorexics, such a person may feel empty inside and binge on food as a substitute for feeling emotionally full. Then, in self-disgust or anger, she purges that feeling by vomiting. Some people feel that this is the easy way to diet. You can eat all you want and never gain a pound. What most people don't realize is that the stomach becomes so used to vomiting that soon it can't ingest anything without it coming right back up. The stomach has to be retrained (like a baby's) to digest soft food and then solids. Some people don't receive the help they need and starve to death because they never get any sustenance. Once again, the core of bulimia is an issue of control. A person who feels as if he has no control over the events in his life thinks that he can control what or how much he eats, but eventually the disorder takes over and the person is too weak to stop.*

In each case food is not the problem. Emotional needs are not being met in healthy ways. The person turns to food, thoughts of food, or actions involving food in vain attempts to fill voids or meet needs. Christians recognize that such emotional needs can be addressed with spiritual assistance and strength that comes from God.

GOD'S WORD (20 MINUTES)

Arrange groups of three to five students. Assign each group one or both Bible passages and sets of questions on the Student Page. Allow them about eight minutes to read and discuss the questions. Then invite volunteers to respond to each Student Page question.

1 Peter 1:18–19—Can any eating or drinking buy long-term popularity or acceptance? Can food or weight measure our worth as a person or guarantee love? What alone can buy (redeem) our souls and bodies? *People with eating disorders use food to express their need for unconditional love and acceptance. They misuse food to meet needs that food can never meet. Only Jesus, the true Bread of Life, can supply all our needs.*

John 6:35–40—Why do you think Jesus uses this bread analogy? *Bread was the basic staple in Jesus' day.*

What is Jesus saying by the words "I am the bread of life"? *In the context of our lesson this verse tells us that Jesus is the basic need, our greatest need.*

How can we help those with eating disorders find alternatives and make choices that bring health and peace? *Be generous with praise and affirmations of ourselves and our friends; do not fake compliments, but look for the value in others and tell them what you see; plan events and fun times that are not centered on food, especially too much food; learn about and refer others to programs or professional counselors if signs of eating disorders appear; introduce them to the Bread of Life, Jesus Christ; pray for them and share the good things God is doing in your life.*

Then say, "Eating disorders are a manifestation of sin in our lives. We all have the basic need to hear and experience God's love and forgiveness. He values each of us so much that He sent His Son, Jesus Christ, to pay our penalties for sin and win victory over Satan and death. As we are strengthened by Christ's presence in our lives through the power of the Holy Spirit, we are empowered to confront the issues of our lives, including eating disorders."

CLOSING (5 MINUTES)

Lead the class in a prayer. Thank God for His many gifts, including His gift of food and His gift of Jesus, the Bread of Life. Ask for God's help, through the Spirit at work in each Christian, to resist eating disorders and help those in need.

5. What's Eating You?

What Would You Do If . . . ?

A friend constantly complains that she is too fat. If anything, she looks as though she should gain 10 or 15 pounds. You have never seen her really eat anything besides a piece of candy here or there, even when out for pizza with everyone. Is there a problem? How do you find out? What do you say to her?

Your friend wrestles and is forever trying to make a lower weight class. He starves himself and even will force himself to vomit if he has eaten too much. He seems to be in good shape, but wrestling season is six months away. Should he be so concerned now? What would you ask him? How can you tell if an eating disorder is involved? What would you do?

Eating Disorders

Food Addiction—A great number of Americans are overweight because they eat as a response to problems and suppress unwanted emotions.

Fat/Thin Disorder—Many people are caught in a cycle of repeatedly overeating and starving themselves.

Anorexia Nervosa—People deliberately starve themselves in response to a distorted self-view or to feelings of losing control in one's life.

Bulimia—A person becomes trapped in a cycle of binge eating and purging.

God's Word

*Read **1 Peter 1:18–19.** Can any eating or drinking buy long-term popularity or acceptance? Can food or weight measure our worth as a person or guarantee love? What alone can buy (redeem) our souls and bodies?*

*Read **John 6:35–40.** Why do you think Jesus uses this bread analogy?*

What is Jesus saying by the words "I am the bread of life"?

How can we help those with eating disorders (including ourselves) find alternatives and make choices that bring health and peace?

getting by without getting high

LESSON FOCUS

Underage drinking seems to be a common experience among teens. Weekend binge-drinking sessions have become commonplace across the nation. Alcohol consumption by teens can have many serious consequences. It frequently contributes to sexual activity, aggression, auto accidents, and alcohol addiction. It ruins many promising lives.

GOSPEL FOCUS

Scripture condemns drunkenness, loss of control, and disobedience to authority. Instead it encourages self-control, primarily as it offers Christ and the power of His forgiveness to meet our spiritual needs and to empower us to live our lives for Him. As God works repentance in our hearts and offers forgiveness, we are empowered to choose alternatives to disobedience, to stand up for those choices, and to minister to others.

Lesson Outline

ACTIVITY	SUGGESTED TIME	MATERIALS NEEDED
Opening	10 minutes	Videotaped alcohol commercials (optional)
Let's Have Some Fun!	10 minutes	Copies of Student Page
Fun without Alcohol?	10 minutes	Bibles
Why Do Youth Drink?	10 minutes	Copies of Student Page
Advice to the King	10 minutes	Chalkboard or newsprint

BEFORE CLASS

Videotape commercials for alcohol from television (sports programs usually have these sponsors). Three or four minutes of commercials should be sufficient.

OPENING (10 MINUTES)

Show the video and ask the class to evaluate each commercial. Ask, "What rationale do the commercials give for drinking? Is their reasoning valid?"

Or ask the students to describe their favorite beer or alcohol commercial or advertisement. Evaluate the claims as suggested above.

LET'S HAVE SOME FUN! (10 MINUTES)

Ask your students for examples of teens they know whose lives have been negatively impacted by alcohol. (You may want to encourage students to use an alias instead of the person's real name. Caution students against gossiping about individuals.) Make a list of some of the tragedies that have happened because of drinking. You could include unwanted sexual activity, aggression, accidents, and addiction.

Divide the class into groups of four to seven students. Ask each group to read the case study and discuss what they might say to Bill. (Or read the story from the Student Page to the whole group before discussion.) Invite summaries from each group.

FUN WITHOUT ALCOHOL? (10 MINUTES)

Ask the students to read Ephesians 5:15–20 one verse at a time. Discuss each verse, using the following questions and comments to guide your discussion.

1. What does it mean to live "not as unwise but as wise" (verse 15)? *To discover what God's will for believers is and to try to live according to it.*

2. St. Paul tells us to make "the most of every opportunity" (verse 16). Opportunity to do what? *To do God's will and serve Him. God's will is that we believe in Jesus as our Savior, trust in Him for forgiveness, and witness His love to everyone—especially to those who do not yet believe. See the Third Petition in Luther's Small Catechism.*

3. Why does the foolish person miss the opportunity to make wise use of his time (verse 17)? *Because the foolish do not understand God's purpose for them in life.*

4. Instead of being filled with spirits (alcohol), the Christian is to be filled with the Holy Spirit. How are these two spirits similar and how are they different? *Both spirits (alcohol) and the Spirit influence a person's behavior. Spirits (alcohol) lead to selfishness and, if consumed in great enough quanti-*

ty, death (physical and spiritual). *The Holy Spirit empowers Christians to do God's will and accomplish His purpose.*

Note: Debauchery is indulgence for pleasure that leads to moral bankruptcy.

5. Drinking spirits (alcohol) results in depression. What is the result of being filled with the Holy Spirit? *Happiness and thanksgiving.*

WHY DO YOUTH DRINK? (10 MINUTES)

Direct the students back into their small groups. Ask them to spend about five minutes discussing this section. Then invite the whole group to start a group list. Use a chalkboard or newsprint to build a list of reasons that young people drink. You may use the reasons discussed at the beginning of the lesson. Below are some possible reasons and corresponding verses from Ephesians chapter 5 related to them. Use these as a guide for your discussion.

1. Association with groups where the ability to hold your liquor is equated with toughness. *"Be very careful, then, how you live—not as unwise" (verse 15).*

2. Desire to conform to peer pressure that says that drinking is the "in" thing to do. *"Therefore do not be foolish" (verse 17).*

3. Boredom or the idea that there's nothing else to do. *"Making the most of every opportunity" (verse 16).*

4. Excitement of doing something wrong without getting caught. *"Which leads to debauchery" (verse 18).*

5. The influence of alcohol allows the youth to feel overly confident. *"Instead, be filled with the Spirit" (verse 18).*

6. An escape from the realities of the world by temporarily numbing the pain. *"Always giving thanks to God the Father for everything" (verse 20).*

7. Reducing inhibitions. Feeling more free to talk, laugh, flirt, or even experiment sexually without your conscience shouting loudly at you.

ADVICE TO THE KING (10 MINUTES)

After reading and briefly discussing the Proverbs passage, have the students help you make a list on a chalkboard, newsprint, or white board of some things that the youth can do in place of drinking alcohol.

Close with a prayer asking for God's forgiveness in Christ for all sins—including those we commit under the influence of alcohol against ourselves and others. Pray that Christians everywhere may be empowered through Word and Sacraments to choose alternatives to alcohol misuse that serve others and give glory to God.

6. Getting by Without Getting High

Let's Have Some Fun!

Bill and David, friends from your class in school, drive up to your house. Bill yells to you through the driver's window, "Hey, I got my driver's license today! Dad let me have the car tonight. Come on, let's cruise the loop."

You jump in the backseat. When the car gets out of sight of your house, David tosses a cold can of beer into your lap. "We've got a whole cooler full of these in the trunk. Are we going to have fun tonight!" What would you say and do?

What if you ask Bill to turn around and take you back home? Bill says, "What's wrong? Don't want to have any fun?" What do you say?

Why Do Youth Drink?

List reasons that youth drink. Where possible, write a verse number from **Ephesians 5:15–20** *that shows the reason you listed to be foolish.*

1. _____

2. _____

3. _____

4. _____

Advice to the King

Read **Proverbs 31:1–7.** *As God in Christ has forgiven us, His Spirit empowers us to choose healthy activities instead of those that would hurt, harm, or otherwise negatively influence us and dishonor Him. List some alternatives to alcohol misuse that would be suitable for King Lemuel and his friends—and you and yours.*

Some ways I can have fun and help my friends have fun without alcohol are . . .

49

7
FINAL EXIT OR THE WRONG DOOR?

LESSON FOCUS

Lack of faith and a misunderstanding of God's purpose for life can result in a person contemplating suicide as a solution to despair, pain, grief, or hopelessness. A person may be more likely to consider suicide if he doubts the reality of eternity or desires relief by escaping difficulties in this present life.

GOSPEL FOCUS

Sin causes us to ignore God and His purpose for our life and to take matters of life and death into our own hands. God forgives us for values and behaviors tainted by sin and offers us hope in the midst of hopelessness and peace in the wake of despair.

Lesson Outline

ACTIVITY	SUGGESTED TIME	MATERIALS NEEDED
Opening	10 minutes	None
Agree or Disagree	10 minutes	Copies of Student Page
Reasons to Die?	10 minutes	Newsprint/paper
A Reason to Live	20 minutes	Chalkboard/newsprint
Closing Activity	5 minutes	None
Bonus Activity	10 minutes	None

AN IMPORTANT NOTE

If at any time in this session a student expresses suicidal comments, take it seriously. Let the student know you are available to listen. Intervene by referring the student for professional help or by making the contact yourself. If a hot line is available in your area for suicide prevention, post the number.

OPENING (10 MINUTES)

Ask students to respond to the questions that follow. Allow them to share freely without evaluating their opinions. Say something such as, "Think of suicides you have seen on television or in movies. Who was it that committed suicide? How did they do it? What were their reasons? How did the scene make you feel? Do you agree or disagree with what the character did?"

Ask, "Are you aware of suicides or suicide attempts by classmates or other people in your community? Do you know why they took place? How do you feel about those experiences?"

AGREE OR DISAGREE (10 MINUTES)

Ask the students to mark the statements in this section of the Student Page. If space allows, you may designate one side of the room as *agree* and the other as *disagree*. Have the students stand on the appropriate side of the room to reflect their opinion as you read each statement. Let students share their reasoning. Then add these insights:

1. Suicide is not the problem. It is a symptom of other problems. *Many experts would agree that suicide is a symptom of problems in a person's life.*

2. Most youth who commit suicide do so in reaction to one bad event, such as breaking up or failing a class. *Although a single event may be the catalyst, most teen suicides are caused by a combination of factors. Many are the result of prolonged depression.*

3. Star athletes, honor students, and members of the popular crowd are in less danger of attempting suicide because they have more to live for. *Suicide affects all kinds of people. Students who appear to have it all together may be the ones who experience the most pressure. They are not immune to the risk of suicide.*

4. Some who attempt suicide don't really want to die. *Many suicide attempts are cries for help. Even those who believe they truly want to die may have mixed feelings.*

5. People who think about suicide or attempt to take their own lives aren't really Christian. *It is clear that the desire to take one's own life is a sin. But we Christians recognize that we all sin daily. Sin does not erase our Christian faith; rather it points out our need for Jesus Christ as Savior.*

6. Suicide can be the best way to resolve some problems. *Most suicides occur because the person can't see a better way out of a problem. Many teens haven't lived long enough to see that things often work out better than their worst fears.*

7. Some people who commit suicide have forgotten how final death is. *Suicide is not temporary. It is a permanent, irreversible end of life.*

8. Suicide is a good way to get back at someone. *Suicide does not cure any problems, nor will it effectively get back at anyone or prove anything.*

9. Suicide is a cruel form of punishment. *Suicide does punish the suicidal person—and others.*

10. Some problems will never be resolved except through suicide. *Life will change and the immediate feelings often pass.*

11. Suicidal people just need to get over it. *Some bodies don't produce the right chemicals to let you cope and feel okay. It's not a sin or unchristian to take an antidepressant.*

REASONS TO DIE? (10 MINUTES)

If possible, divide your class into two or more groups of three to five students. Ask each group to brainstorm a list of responses to the question "What kinds of circumstances might lead someone to commit suicide?" Think of situations or events that may lead someone to believe he or she has a reason to die. Give each group a sheet of newsprint or paper to record their lists. Let the groups share their lists.

Ask students to evaluate the items on their list realistically. Ask, "What are positive ways to deal with the situations or events we have listed?" Stress that suicide is a permanent solution to a temporary problem.

A REASON TO LIVE (20 MINUTES)

Direct the group to the quote on the Student Page. Then say, "In the midst of hopelessness and despair, Jesus invites us: 'Come to Me, all you who are weary and burdened, and I will give you rest' (Matthew 11:28). When lack of faith leads us to make unwise choices or creates a desire to harm ourselves, we can look to Jesus. Even while dying on a cross, Jesus intercedes on our behalf, 'Father, forgive them' (Mark 23:34). Through His resurrection Jesus proclaims victory for us over sin, over death, and over the power of the devil. When in faith we look to Jesus for help, we can be sure that nothing can separate us from His love."

Divide again into groups and assign one of the Scripture sections to each. Write the following questions on a chalkboard or on newsprint:

* What hope is there for someone who is afraid of living?

* Do these verses answer the question "Why did this happen to me?" How do you answer that question from a friend?

* What specifically does our faith in Christ give us in times of despair?

Give the groups time to discuss their verses by using the questions. Then ask them to summarize their verses and the hope they find in them with the whole class.

Reread Romans 8:37–39. Ask the students to fill in the blanks with situations in their own lives that may cause them to feel depressed or hopeless. Let students share if they wish. Accept all student responses. What seems insignificant to you may be a serious issue for a young person. Reaffirm that we are never without hope in Jesus Christ and that nothing can separate us from His love. Jesus lived, died, and rose to give us reason to live.

CLOSING (5 MINUTES)

As you lead the class in a closing prayer, provide a time of silence for students to pray about their own or others' seemingly hopeless situations. Then ask the Lord to give renewed hope in the knowledge that nothing will separate us from His love.

Bonus Activity

Have each student choose one of the items they have listed under the "Reasons to Die?" section and write a letter to an imaginary young person who is experiencing that problem.

7. Suicide: Final Exit or the Wrong Door?

Agree or Disagree

1. Suicide is not the problem. It is a symptom of other problems.
2. Most youth who commit suicide do so in reaction to one bad event, such as breaking up or failing a class.
3. Star athletes, honor students, and members of the popular crowd are in less danger of attempting suicide because they have more to live for.
4. Some who attempt suicide don't really want to die.
5. People who think about suicide or attempt to take their own lives aren't really Christian.
6. Suicide can be the best way to resolve some problems.
7. Some people who commit suicide have forgotten how final death is.
8. Suicide is a good way to get back at someone.
9. Suicide is a cruel form of punishment.
10. Some problems will never be resolved except through suicide.
11. Suicidal people just need to get over it.

Reasons to Die?

What kinds of circumstances might lead someone to commit suicide? Think of situations or events that may lead someone to believe he or she has a reason to die. Make a list on newsprint or on the back of this page.

A Reason to Live

"Suicide is not so much the desire to die as it is the fear of living."

Read the passages below and share how they offer God's hope in a hopeless situation.

Romans 8:18–25, 31–32   **2 Corinthians 4:1, 5–12**   **Romans 8:37–39**

No, in all these things we are more than conquerors through Him who loved us. For I am convinced that neither _____ nor _____, neither _____ nor _____, neither _____ nor _____, nor any _____, neither _____ nor _____, nor anything else in all creation, will be able to separate us from the love of God that is in Christ Jesus our Lord.

49

8 REAL ANGRY

anger

LESSON FOCUS

Anger is real. God built this emotion into us at the time of creation. Anger in itself is not bad. How we express our anger can be sinful. Uncontrolled anger can hurt feelings and destroy relationships.

GOSPEL FOCUS

Through Christ, God restores our broken relationship with Him, forgives us when we hurt others in our anger, and enables us to direct our anger in appropriate ways.

Lesson Outline

ACTIVITY	SUGGESTED TIME	MATERIALS NEEDED
As Students Arrive	Before class	Newspapers
My Anger	5 minutes	Copies of Student Page, newsprint, markers
God's Anger	20 minutes	Copies of Student Page, Bibles
How Will I Handle My Anger?	15 minutes	Copies of Student Page, Bibles
My Personal Contract	5 minutes	Copies of Student Page
Closing	5 minutes	Paper, markers

AS STUDENTS ARRIVE (BEFORE CLASS)

Gather newspaper articles related to anger—crimes, protests, demonstrations, and so forth. Post the articles on the walls or bulletin boards around the room. Greet students as they arrive. Allow time for students to examine the articles. Informally discuss the news reports with students. Ask, "Were the actions appropriate? Have you ever been angry enough to participate in a protest? Have you ever hurt someone out of anger?"

MY ANGER (5 MINUTES)

Call the class together and distribute copies of the Student Page. Direct students to the "My Anger" situations listed on the Student Page. You may want to add students' ideas to this list. Write them on a chalkboard or newsprint. Once you have developed a list of four or five additional items, have the participants choose the situation that makes them most angry and explain the reason for their choice. Try an expressive voting technique. Ask students to shake their fists, growl, or stomp their feet to indicate their choice.

Or ask, "Have you ever counted to 10 when you were angry? How far would you have to count if (read the situation)?" Tabulate the results. Assure students that righteous anger is okay. Anger is an emotion. What we often do with our anger, however, can become a sin.

GOD'S ANGER (20 MINUTES)

Form small groups of four to seven students. Instruct each group to read the Scripture references and then discuss the questions that follow. After groups have finished, call everyone back together and ask each group to share what they discovered.

Exodus 32:7–10

Who is angry? *The verses speak of God's anger over the sins of the people of Israel.*

Why? *God never sins and condemns all sin. (See Romans 6:23.)*

Was the anger proper considering the situation? *Yes, the people had disobeyed God.*

Do you think God is angry about your sin? Why or why not? *Yes. While God loves the sinner, He despises sin.*

Romans 5:6–11

Although angry over our sin, what did God do for all people? *He sent Jesus Christ into this world to suffer and die for all sinners so they might receive complete forgiveness of sin, including the sinful use of anger.*

Who receives the benefits from God's action? *Repentant sinners receive the blessings Christ earned—forgiveness and eternal life.*

How do we respond to God's action on our behalf? *Student answers will vary.*

HOW WILL I HANDLE MY ANGER? (15 MINUTES)

Direct students to the third part of the lesson. Tell them, "God's forgiveness in Christ empowers us to use our anger in God-pleasing ways. In Proverbs God provides King Solomon with wisdom about anger. Read the passages and then write some guidelines for anger." Allow students to work in small groups or independently. Through God's Word and Sacraments, He strengthens us to serve Him. The Holy Spirit enables us to control our anger. Guidelines could include these ideas: "Use gentle words. Do not let your anger get out of control. Out-of-control anger causes dissension. Do not remain angry with someone."

MY PERSONAL CONTRACT (5 MINUTES)

Ask the students to complete the personal contract based on the information they gained from the previous activity. A sample response might be, "With God's help I will try to focus on the situation and not the people involved."

CLOSING (5 MINUTES)

Read Ephesians 4:26–27. Then form the students back into small groups. Ask each group to create a slogan based on these verses or other passages studied during this session. Sample slogans might include "Don't go to bed mad" or "In Christ, Christians can love one another—even when it's tough." Ask each group to share its slogan. Close with a brief prayer. Point out that as God forgives us, we are empowered to forgive others, even those with whom we get angry.

8. Real Angry

my anger

Choose a situation below that makes you angry, or list one or more of your personal hot buttons.

A parent who says no to something I really want to do.

A friend who knowingly lets me down or disappoints me.

A teacher who treats me unfairly.

Seeing other people suffer unjustly.

Unexpected happenings that interrupt my plans.

god's anger

Read **Exodus 32:7–10.**

Who is angry?

Why?

Was the anger proper considering the situation?

Do you think God is angry about your sin? Why or why not?

Romans 5:6–11

Although angry over our sin, what did God do for all people?

Who receives the benefits from God's action? (See John 1:8–9.)

How do we respond to God's action on our behalf?

anger

hOW WiLL i hANdLE MY ANGER?

Read the following: **Proverbs 15:1; 29:11; 29:22.**

Form some guidelines for handling anger, using the ideas included in the passages.

Guideline—

Guideline—

Guideline—

MY PERSONAL CONTRACT

With God's help, when I get angry I will try to . . .

i'm boRed!

LESSON FOCUS

In an age of high technology and constant sensory stimulation, young people may complain of frequent boredom or become trapped in a quest for ever-increasing excitement. They may look for fun rather than meaningful relationships and activities.

GOSPEL FOCUS

Recreation and exciting leisure-time activities are not in themselves sinful. They become sinful when they are self-centered, crowding out thoughts and actions that would honor God or meet the needs of others. God in His love for us sent Jesus to rescue us from our sin and motivates us to honor Him with our words and actions.

Lesson Outline

ACTIVITY	SUGGESTED TIME	MATERIALS NEEDED
Me and My Free Time	10 minutes	Copies of Student Page
My Typical Free-Time Activities	10 minutes	Newsprint, markers, copies of Student Page
What Scripture Says	20 minutes	Copies of Student Page, Bibles
Expanding My List	5 minutes	Copies of Student Page
Prayers for Forgiveness	15 minutes	Newsprint and markers or blank paper
Bonus Opening	15 minutes	Newsprint or chalkboard, blank paper
Bonus Activity	10 minutes	Bibles

BEFORE CLASS

Review your own use of leisure time. Pray for God's guidance as you apply the objectives for this session in your own life. Pray specifically for any students that you suspect or know are using their leisure time in especially self-destructive behaviors.

ME AND MY FREE TIME (10 MINUTES)

Distribute copies of the Student Page. Ask, "If you had this Saturday free to do anything you wanted, what would you do?" Limit responses to activities that are genuinely possible. Have students write their thoughts as indicated on the Student Page. Have students share their choices with a partner. Then ask students to introduce their partners, sharing their name and telling what their partner would do with their free Saturday.

When all students are introduced, lead the group in prayer. Ask God to bless today's study of His Word as you talk about leisure.

Do You Have Time? (Bonus Opening)

Distribute a sheet of blank paper to each student. Then say, "'Do you have time?' How often are you asked that question? The answer of course is, 'Yes.' We all have time. God gives each of us the gift of 24 hours each day to invest. How do you spend your typical 168-hour week? And what kinds of returns are you getting on your time investments?"

Invite the class to share some of the typical activities in which people regularly invest their time (sleeping, working, doing laundry, etc.). Record their answers on newsprint or the chalkboard. Then instruct students to make a three-column chart on their blank sheets of paper. Label the first column Activity, *the second* Time Investment, *and the third* Returns. *Tell the class to use any of the typical activities from the class list as well as additional activities in which they invest their time. Fill in the chart.*

Allow about five minutes for students to create and fill in their charts. Then divide the class into groups of three to five students. Appoint a person in each group to serve as leader. Each group member is to evaluate briefly the returns he gets on his time investments. Group members may determine, for instance, that they are or are not satisfied with what they reap from their time investments. Or they may have difficulty recognizing any benefit from a particular activity. Reconvene the class. Ask a reporter from each group to share an overview of what group members discovered.

MY TYPICAL FREE-TIME ACTIVITIES (10 MINUTES)

Have students fill in their typical free-time activities for this time of year in the table on the Student Page. While they work individually, distribute sheets of newsprint and markers around the room so that there is one newsprint sheet and one marker for every three or four students. Ask students to gather in groups of three or four and compile on newsprint a composite list of their group's typical free-time activities. Suggest that within each group students share one idea at a time until all ideas are listed.

Ask the groups to present their lists to the class. As they listen to the lists, have students add activities to their personal lists that they might have originally overlooked. Then have students attach a percentage to each item (using the percentage column of the table) so that the total of the percentages equals one hundred percent of their free time.

Then ask, "What patterns do you see in your use of free time?" Among the likely comments may be surprise at the variety, comments on the merits of particular activities, or confessions to a lot of doing nothing or wasted time. Accept all responses at this time. Encourage students to be open and honest.

WHAT SCRIPTURE SAYS (20 MINUTES)

Have everyone find Luke 12:16–21 in their Bible. Invite a volunteer to read the story aloud. Then direct the students to work through the questions on the Student Page in their small groups. After about 10 minutes invite reports from the small groups. Use the following comments to assist you as you lead discussion.

1. How was the rich man in this parable sinful? *It is not a sin to be wealthy or to enjoy life. The essence of the rich man's sin was in his idolatry of self and pleasure.*

2. Was his sin more an action or an attitude? Why? *In reality, the rich man sinned in both a self-centered attitude and selfish actions. Remind students that sinful attitudes create as much difficulty for us as sinful actions, because actions result from attitudes.*

3. What connection is there between this story told by Jesus and our use of free time? *God does not condemn eating, drinking (in moderation for those of legal age), and enjoyment (Jesus turned water into wine for a wedding banquet). He does not desire that our lives be void of pleasure. To the contrary, God seeks to give us abundant life. God condemns the idolatry of putting personal pleasure ahead of Him and His will for our lives.*

4. Is it ever all right to eat, drink, and be merry? *God desires that we enjoy life. When the eating, drinking, and being merry excludes God or becomes the most important thing in our lives, we sin against the First Commandment.*

5. What does it mean to be rich toward God? *To be rich toward God involves humility (acknowledging that God is the source of wealth and prosperity), faith (trusting God to care for us regardless of our socioeconomic standing), and service (using wealth responsibly for the good of others and the growth of God's kingdom). Emphasize that God made us rich in Him through His Son's sacrificial death on the cross.*

Have students place a check mark in the left column beside any free-time activities on the Student Page that tend to reflect richness toward God. Then have them add the percentages of all the checked activities. After most have finished, ask if they've discovered anything new about their use of free time. Follow up with these questions.

"What makes any of our free-time activities sinful or unhealthy?" *Answers could include timing (if you're supposed to be doing something else); the activity itself could be unlawful (using drugs, underage drinking, and so forth); or the activities could be motivated by selfishness.*

"Is it ever okay to use free time just for ourselves?" *Yes. We all need time to ourselves to catch our breath and be refreshed. Even Jesus often took time to be alone to be refreshed and restored (Matthew 14:13, 23; Luke 5:16; 6:12).*

How to Spend Time (Bonus Activity)

Tell students that St. Paul has a message for us as Christians concerning the use of our time. Have the class locate and read aloud together Ephesians 5:15–21. Remind students that we desire to do what pleases God because He loved us and sent Jesus to suffer and die for us. What does the verse say about

- wasting time? (See verse 16.) *Leisure time is not wasted time, especially as we rest in the Lord. Even in our leisure activities we can still let our faith show.*

- staying spiritually focused? (See verse 17.) *Just because we're relaxing from work does not mean we relax from obedience to God's will.*

- being clear-headed? (See verse 18.) *In order to be alert to God's hand and voice in our lives, we can't afford to dull and confuse our minds with harmful or excessive use of drugs or alcohol.*

- being bored? (See verse 19.) *There is always something to do in Christ—sing a song of praise, write a poem of praise, or find your own way to talk to Him or about Him.*

- complaining and feeling sorry for oneself? (See verse 20.) *No matter what our circumstances in life, bitterness and complaining never resolve anything. We can instead focus on what God has done for us.*

- being inconsiderate? (See verse 21.) *In choosing our leisure activities, we consider how our actions affect other people.*

EXPANDING MY LIST (5 MINUTES)

Have students fill in the two blanks in the bottom box of their Student Page with the phrase *Serve God*. Brainstorm with the whole group things they could do, together or individually, the next time they find themselves saying, "I'm bored." List the ideas on a chalkboard or newsprint. Ask for individuals to tell about a time they did one of these and how it felt. Have students write one or more of these ideas in the space provided at the bottom of the Student Page.

PRAYERS FOR FORGIVENESS (15 MINUTES)

Remind the students of the parable of the forgiving father/prodigal son (Luke 15:11–32). The prodigal son was forgiven after squandering away his entire life. God provides complete forgiveness to us through faith in Jesus for the times we've sinfully used free time, as well as all other sins.

Choose one of the following options.

Have the small groups write on newsprint a prayer for forgiveness based on Luke 12:16–21. Then have the class read the prayers together.

Or have individuals write a prayer asking forgiveness for their misuse of free time and seeking God's strength for more selfless attitudes and actions. Invite them to share their prayers in pairs, small groups, with the entire group, or in a time of silent prayer.

IF YOU HAVE MORE TIME

Plan a group service project. Discuss where you would serve, when you could go, what service you could provide, what adult leadership would be needed, and who could provide it. Investigate servant events that are organized by your national church office.

9. "i'm bored!"

me and my free time

If I could do anything I wanted this Saturday, I would . . .

My Typical Free-Time Activities

What scripture says

Read *Luke 12:16–21*.

1. How was the rich man in this parable sinful?

2. Was his sin more an action or an attitude? Why?

3. What connection is there between this story told by Jesus and our use of free time?

4. Is it ever all right to eat, drink, and be merry?

5. What does it mean to be rich toward God?

expanding my list . . .

10

what should i do?

LESSON FOCUS

One of the big decisions facing most high school students is "Where will I go next?" College, vocational school, military service, and joining the workforce are all options. College is frequently seen as the ideal, with others being second rate. As God has uniquely gifted and blessed each person, such a choice is best made based on "Where can I best serve Him?"

GOSPEL FOCUS

Through prayer, discussion with parents and others, and thoughtful deliberation, God leads Christian young people to make wise choices. He promises to support us with the power of His Spirit working through the Word and Sacraments as we seek to do His will.

Lesson Outline

ACTIVITY	SUGGESTED TIME	MATERIALS NEEDED
Decisions	10 minutes	Copies of Student Page, newsprint or chalkboard
Options on the Future	15 minutes	Newsprint or marker board
Gifts for the Future	15 minutes	Copies of Student Page, Bibles
With the Spirit's Help	15 minutes	Copies of Student Page, Bibles
Closing	5 minutes	None

DECISIONS (10 MINUTES)

Distribute copies of the Student Page and pencils or pens. Direct students to prepare a list of the big decisions they have made. Seed the process with some examples that are realistic for your group (what clothes to buy or wear, what classes to take this year in school, whom to take to the dance, what friends to have).

After a couple of minutes invite volunteers to share their responses and compile a list on newsprint or the board for all to see. Then ask them to think about which decisions have had the most impact on their lives. Invite a few volunteers to share their response. Then say, "For most of you, many of your biggest decisions lie in the future. Some of them will be made in the next few years. In this study we'll look at one of those decisions—what will you do after high school? Will it be college or career? What kind of study? What kind of work? Let's begin the process with prayer."

Lead the group in a prayer similar to this one: "Dear Lord, You promise to lead and support Your people. Guide us in our decisions about the future. Help us make wise choices that will serve You and Your kingdom. Help us to say as Your Son, Jesus, did, 'Not as I will, but as You will.' In His name we pray. Amen."

OPTIONS ON THE FUTURE (15 MINUTES)

Ask the class to brainstorm any and all possible directions that the students could take after high school. Record their responses on newsprint or a marker board. Remind the students to avoid mental editing while doing this. Keep the brainstorming free and open. Possibilities include college, work, technical school, military service, marriage, and the Peace Corps. When ideas slow down, encourage listing more specific types in broad categories: Army, Navy, Marines, plumber, doctor, bus driver, secretary, etc. Strive for 10 or 20 examples.

Take time at this point to talk about the biases that exist in this society about professions and career choices. Caution your students that the value society assigns an occupation or profession may not reflect the real value of the individuals, created by God, who do that work. Remind the students that we should keep an open mind about various life callings.

If you have time, you might discuss one or two examples of frequently stereotyped occupations (such as lawyers or librarians), the unfair judgments that we sometimes make, and the sources of our bias.

GIFTS FOR THE FUTURE (15 MINUTES)

Read or have a volunteer read James 1:5, 16–18 aloud as the students follow along in their Bibles. After the reading is finished, focus on the passage "Every good and perfect gift is from above" (verse 17). Remind the class that all good and useful talents, gifts, and interests are truly God-given, reflecting great diversity among people. Just as God has made each individual unique in physical form and appearance, so God has given each person unique gifts of the spirit and intellect to use for making a living, helping others, and serving God. Since it is really God who equips us for life, each person should prayerfully ask himself or herself, "Where can I best serve? How can I best serve?" Request that each student spend a couple of minutes contemplating his or her strengths and talents, and also ask students to write two or three of them down on the Student Page in the space provided. Next to each entry have the student list occupations where each talent might be profitably used. Ask them to write how this gift might be used to directly or indirectly serve God's purposes—especially through touching the lives of others.

Allow time for sharing in groups of threes. Or invite volunteers to share their responses with the class. If your students seem reluctant to brag about themselves, allow them to suggest strengths and talents for one another. For example, Chandra may be friendly and outgoing, a useful trait of politicians, salespeople, or store clerks. Jon may be caring and thoughtful, making him suited for counseling, medical practice, or child care. Stress that students should find and consider lots of options. Point out that every occupation can serve God in many ways.

One resource for the students is the PSAT, which is now included in most high school testing or counseling cycles. Many high schools feature an annual Career Day on their school calendars. This is another ideal opportunity for students to gather brochures and to speak with representatives of the local, regional, or national business sectors. Field trips to nearby colleges and universities are also available through most high schools. Christian colleges can be an excellent alternative to secular universities. They are frequently smaller, more intimate, and have a more positive environment for learning life skills and bringing the student closer to God, instead of enticing the student away. The Concordia University System trains students to be professional church workers (pastors, teachers, directors of Christian education, directors of Christian outreach, deaconesses, directors of parish music, and the like). The Concordia University System also trains students for countless other professions in a Lutheran Christian environment.

WITH THE SPIRIT'S HELP (15 MINUTES)

Decisions are not made in a vacuum; they require time, research, discussion, and prayer. Relate to the students one decision you struggled with during your teenage years. How did you feel then? Whom did you talk to? What mistakes did you make? What did you do right? Advise the students to seek out older adults who can be trusted as a source of wisdom: parents, high school/college counselors, businesspeople, professionals, pastors, or laypeople in the congregation. Remind the class about Christ struggling with His future in the Garden of Gethsemane, of God's will and Christ's submission, and that we are never alone in this world as we confront the uncertainty of the future. Christ has promised to help and support us through the Holy Spirit. Ask the class to turn to Luke 11:9–13. After reading the verses, ask students to write down how they or their family have been guided and blessed by the Holy Spirit in past decision-making. Give students time to write a brief prayer.

CLOSING (5 MINUTES)

Ask the class to form into pairs. Have each share with the other his or her concerns, cares, and dilemmas regarding the future. Then ask students to pray for their partner. Or invite volunteers to share the prayers they have written.

10. What Should I do?

decisions

List four big decisions you have made so far in life.

gifts for the future

What skills, talents, and personal traits has God given you that could be a significant focus in your future? Write at least two or three in the space below. Next to each one, list one or more occupations or future activities where that gift might be useful. Finally, describe how this gift might be used to touch others with God's love through you.

With the Spirit's help

*Read **Luke 11:9–13**. The Holy Spirit is a powerful source of wisdom and strength for God's people and was sent to the disciples after Christ's ascension. The Spirit enabled the disciples to boldly carry on Christ's commission on earth after Pentecost. Think about how the Spirit has guided you, members of your family, or others you know in making decisions. Describe how God blessed a decision through the Spirit's power.*

Knowing it is God's will to bless those who ask for good gifts that reflect His will, write a brief prayer asking God to guide and bless the decisions you make about the future.

11

managing my time and myself

LESSON FOCUS

Many young people find themselves caught in schedules rivaling those of the busiest adults. They struggle to find time for work, school, and friends—and time for personal devotions and church activities gets squeezed out. At the heart of their struggle is the reality that each person experiences the same 24-hour day and many of the same choices. In light of God's Word and enabled by His grace, we all can evaluate and adjust our personal priorities.

GOSPEL FOCUS

Typical time-management strategies focus on personal effort and tips for using time more efficiently—squeezing more "stuff" into already hectic lives. Such efforts, unless informed by God's Word and preceded by honest evaluation of priorities, are doomed to the failure inherent in our human nature. God in Christ forgives us for our unwise use of time and empowers us by Christ's love to make wise choices.

Lesson Outline

ACTIVITY	SUGGESTED TIME	MATERIALS NEEDED
Opening	10 minutes	Index cards or newsprint and markers
Time to Evaluate My Priorities	10 minutes	Copies of Student Page
Time to Look at God's Word	15 minutes	Copies of Student Page, Bibles
Time to Make Adjustments	10 minutes	Copies of Student Page
Closing	15 minutes	Bibles
Bonus Activity	10 minutes	None

OPENING (10 MINUTES)

Before class, write each of the 10 questions listed below on separate note cards. Have students take turns drawing one card, reading it, and answering its question aloud. If there are more than 10 students, cards should be returned and reused.

1. If you could live in another time, tell when and why.

2. Tell what you might be doing when an hour goes so fast for you that it's over before you know it.

3. Tell what you might be doing when an hour goes so slow for you that it seems to last forever.

4. Tell what your favorite hour of the day is and why.

5. Tell what your favorite day of the week is and why.

6. Tell what your favorite time of year is and why.

7. Tell what you'd do if you had one extra free hour every day.

8. Tell what you would give up doing if you had one less hour each day.

9. Tell what you'd do if you had one extra free day every week.

10. Tell what your least favorite time of the year is and why.

Or divide students into two groups. Give each group a marker and a large piece of poster board or newsprint. Have Group One list words and phrases that describe someone with good time-management skills (reliable, prompt, etc.). Have Group Two list words and phrases that describe someone with poor time-management skills (procrastinates, wastes time, etc.). Set a timer for five minutes and challenge students to list as many words as possible before the timer buzzes. Post the lists and ask, "Which words and phrases describe *you*?"

TIME TO EVALUATE MY PRIORITIES (10 MINUTES)

Say, "These days it seems we're all busy—too busy. Raise your hand if you are someone who somehow squeezes everything in; says, 'Maybe it'll get done; maybe it won't'; organizes and plans ahead; or puts things off to the last minute." Take time to get responses. Invite volunteers to explain their answers. Ask, "Are you satisfied with your answer?"

Then say, "Raise your hand if you think time management is something you do pretty well, but there's room for improvement; you do very well, so it's really not an issue for you; or you really don't think about because things just seem to get done. Would you say, 'Time management? Who has time for it?' Or are you someone who can't seem to get a grip on time?"

Distribute copies of the Student Page. Encourage students to be honest as they complete the first exercise on the priorities in their lives. Allow them to share their top three priorities with two or three others in a small group.

TIME TO LOOK AT GOD'S WORD (15 MINUTES)

With the students still in their small groups, direct them to complete and share their responses to the three discussion questions in this section. After about 10 minutes, invite small groups to report on their discussion. Add the following comments as students share their responses.

> 1. Read Matthew 6:24–34 and Colossians 3:1–3. What are God's top priorities? *God's priorities are our salvation and our welfare. When we invest time in worrying or let our priorities get out of whack, we are doomed to failure. God desires us to trust in Him and His help for all our daily needs. Emphasize God's forgiveness in Jesus Christ for our failure to set our hearts on things above. Emphasize how God's love in Christ enables us to start all over again, motivated to establish priorities that reflect His will.*

> 2. What does it mean to seek first His kingdom, and how does this influence the choices we make in our use of time? *When we seek first His kingdom, we put God first in our lives. All our other choices will reflect Him as our number-one priority.*

> 3. With so many choices and demands on our time, how can we accomplish all that needs to be done? See Zechariah 4:6; 1 Peter 5:7; and Matthew 7:7–8. *When we keep in mind God's priorities and seek His help, the Holy Spirit strengthens us to make wise choices in our use of time.*

TIME TO MAKE ADJUSTMENTS (10 MINUTES)

Refer students to the list of priorities under "Time to Evaluate My Priorities." Ask them to identify any priorities that need adjustment and to choose one to work on during the following week. Have them write this priority at the bottom of the Student Page and list practical steps they can take to meet this commitment. (The first step, pray for God's help, is already listed.)

CLOSING (15 MINUTES)

Ask students to share stories about times they have had to make tough choices between priorities and their use of time. What choices did they make? What helped them get through the tough times? Would they handle the situation differently if they could do it all over again? Be ready to share some of your own struggles (and successes) with time management and personal priorities.

Ask students to read aloud Ecclesiastes 3:1–14 together. Follow with a period of silence for students to pray privately for God's help and guidance as they work on their personal priorities and time management.

Bonus Activity

Read each of the descriptions below to the class. Ask students to keep in mind their personal priorities as they consider the choices to be made in each instance.

1. Your friends plan to go out for a late movie and pizza on Saturday night. You're supposed to be at church at 5:00 A.M. to help with the Easter breakfast. What do you do? Explain why.

2. You need a job to start saving money for college. You get an offer at a restaurant. They tell you the job is yours if you can work Sunday mornings. Do you take the job? Why or why not?

3. You have an English paper due tomorrow morning and a major test in history class. You have a youth group meeting at church. Your mom wants you to drive your younger sister to and from piano lessons before your meeting. What do you do?

Remind students that their faith is strengthened through Word and Sacraments, where the Holy Spirit can enable them to make wise, God-first choices in their lives.

II. managing my time and myself

time to evaluate my priorities

What's important to you at this point in your life?
Rank these priorities 1 (most important) through 8 (least important).

____ *family*

____ *recreation/exercise*

____ *friends*

____ *social activities*

____ *God/church*

____ *school/education*

____ *hobbies/special interests*

____ *work*

time to look at god's word

*1. Read **Matthew 6:24–34** and **Colossians 3:1–3.** What are God's top priorities?*

2. What does it mean to seek first His kingdom, and how does this influence the choices we make in our use of time?

*3. With so many choices and demands on our time, how can we accomplish all that needs to be done? (See **Zechariah 4:6; 1 Peter 5:7;** and **Matthew 7:7–8.**)*

time to make adjustments

Look back at the list of priorities above. Which one(s) need to be adjusted? Choose one to work on and list steps you can take to achieve this goal.

I'm making a commitment to work on _____.

Things I can do to make this priority a reality in my life include the following:

1.   Praying for God's help.

2.   _____.

3.   _____.

LESSON FOCUS

God created them male and female. The differences between guys and girls was an intentional part of His plan. They differ not just physically, but also in the way they think and in the way they feel. Because of sin, we often consider differences as occasions for put-downs and stereotyping, with all the pain, hurt, and misunderstanding that they cause. Young people will better appreciate and understand one another as they learn to affirm their differences.

GOSPEL FOCUS

In faith Christ unites all believers, both male and female. He calls them to support, care for, and appreciate the uniqueness of each of His creations.

As we grow through the Word, God's Holy Spirit enables us to celebrate those differences and to affirm one another.

LESSON OUTLINE

ACTIVITY	SUGGESTED TIME	MATERIALS NEEDED
Opening	5 minutes	None
Pop Quiz	20 minutes	Copies of Student Page
What Scripture Says	10 minutes	Bible, paper, board or newsprint
What Scripture Says to Me	10 minutes	Copies of Student Page
Closing	5 minutes	None

OPENING (5 MINUTES)

Introduce the lesson using the "Lesson Focus" paragraph. Open with a brief prayer that (1) recognizes that God made us all, both male and female; (2) thanks God for the plan He designed for males and females to appreciate, complement, and support one another; (3) asks God to help us show openness to each other as males and females and to listen to each other; and (4) places our discussion in His hands.

77

THE POP QUIZ (20 MINUTES)

Ask participants to fill out the quiz individually, withholding their comments until everyone has completed the 12 questions. Then work through each question briefly, asking students how many chose true, false, or not sure. (Only questions 6 and 12 are factually true; all others are a matter of individual experience or opinion. Thus, not sure would be most appropriate.)

Make this point as you discuss the quiz: "While there are some factual differences between males and females, much of the perceived differences are a matter of individual gifts, talents, and abilities." When you sense a somewhat equally divided opinion among the group, ask individuals of one opinion to each find a person of the opposite view and spend three minutes explaining to each other just why they made the choice they did.

After two or three such discussions, bring the whole group back together and ask them to make a summary statement of what they are learning about differences. Write their suggestions on a chalkboard or newsprint.

WHAT SCRIPTURE SAYS (10 MINUTES)

Form your class into groups of four to seven students. Ask the participants to read the Scripture passages and write a one-sentence summary of each, describing the unique characteristics each person may have. Provide a sheet of paper, or ask students to use the back of the Student Page.

Assign one or more of these texts to each group: Genesis 1:26–28; 2:18–25; 1 Corinthians 12:1–11; 12:12–27; Colossians 3:11–14; and Philippians 2:1–4.

As each text is read, ask each group member to write his or her own summary. When the groups are finished, ask them to share their summaries. Allow volunteers to share their summaries with the whole group.

Affirm the following key concepts:

* *Genesis 1:26–28 Male and female created in God's image. Both are blessed and given responsibilities.*

Genesis 2:18–25 Man and woman were created for each other. God Himself established marriage.

1 Corinthians 12:1–11 God gives a great variety of gifts through His Spirit. The gifts are given for the good of all. God gives each the precise gifts He wants them to have.

1 Corinthians 12:12–27 God's people need one another—each one is a vital part of God's design.

Colossians 3:11–14 God calls us to be caring, compassionate people. Through the forgiveness that Christ made available to us through His life, death, and resurrection, He empowers us to be loving and forgiving toward others.

Philippians 2:1–4 As God works faith in us, we show this faith in the way we deal with people, regarding others as better than ourselves and placing the interests of others ahead of our own.

WHAT SCRIPTURE SAYS TO ME (10 MINUTES)

Direct the students to this section of the Student Page. Use your knowledge of your class to determine whether to have students share their responses in this section. If your students have been together as a group and are able to share some reasonably serious things with one another in class without getting chuckles, let them know that you will ask them to share the last two responses with the group. If you're not sure the group is ready to share something this personal, then assure them that these last two items are for their eyes only. The items will serve as opportunities for them to reflect on the day's study.

Then proceed to introduce the first item in your own words. Give them time to think and write before going on to item two.

Have the students share their responses according to your choice above—in small groups or in the group as a whole.

CLOSING (5 MINUTES)

Lead the group in a closing prayer that (1) thanks God for the gift of maleness and femaleness, (2) thanks Him for the time spent together in the Word, (3) asks forgiveness for all for the times we ignore one another's gifts, and (4) asks for the Spirit's blessing as we continue to live, work, study, love, and live together as men and women.

For additional resource and Bible studies on the issue of gender differences, see *Guy Stuff/Girl Stuff—Maturing In Christ* (CPH item #20-3232) and *Guy Stuff/Girl Stuff—Dating and Sexuality* (CPH item # 20-3272).

12. hey, we're different!

POP QUIZ

(Circle T for True, F for False, or NS for Not Sure.)

For the most part, females . . .

1. T F NS . . . *are more emotional than males.*

2. T F NS . . . *are more serious students.*

3. T F NS . . . *care more about personality than looks in the people they date.*

4. T F NS . . . *are best suited for the caring professions—nursing, teaching, etc.*

5. T F NS . . . *are better managers of their time than most males.*

6. T F NS . . . *will outlive most men their same age.*

For the most part, males . . .

7. T F NS . . . *care more about looks than personality in the people they date.*

8. T F NS . . . *have large egos, and their pride is easily wounded.*

9. T F NS . . . *think more about sex in a relationship with a female than about the person.*

10. T F NS . . . *are best suited for the technical professions— engineers, computer analysts, architects, etc.*

11. T F NS . . . *are not very sensitive or caring individuals.*

12. T F NS . . . *are physically stronger than most females.*

What Scripture says to me

1. The truth about the uniqueness of males and females that seems most significant to me at this time in my life is . . .

2. One thing I need to work on with God's help in this whole area is . . .

gender differences